BRAIN

prayers

Explore
Your
Brain

Expand
Your
Prayers

Karen D. Wood

WestBow Press books may be ordered through booksellers or by contacting:

WestBow Press
A Division of Thomas Nelson & Zondervan
1663 Liberty Drive
Bloomington, IN 47403
www.westbowpress.com
1 (866) 928-1240

ISBN: 978-1-4908-3362-0 (sc)
ISBN: 978-1-4908-3363-7 (e)

Library of Congress Control Number: 2014907581

Printed in the United States of America.

WestBow Press rev. date: 5/9/2014

WESTBOW°
PRESS
A DIVISION OF THOMAS NELSON
& ZONDERVAN

contents

brain map

frontal lobes
pages 43-48

parietal lobe

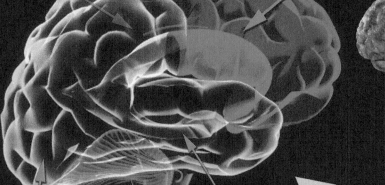

cortex =
the grey
matter on
the outside
of the brain

temporal
lobe
pages 31-36

occipital lobe
pages 37-42

outside

lobes = areas of the brain related to function

thalamus
pages 7-12

cingulate gyrus
pages 19-24

corpus
collosum
pages 25-30

LIMBIC
SYSTEM

amygdala
pages 1-6

hippocampus
pages 13-18

brain stem
pages 49-54

inside

why this book on

Brain Prayers:
explore and learn much
more about the brain, and
expand the power of
praying "outside the box"
for the brain.

What is gained from learning about the brain?

+ The brain is our operating system, and yet we know so little about how we operate!

+ Learning about the functions and systems in the brain allows us to understand so much more about how the past has created our brains, why we do what we do, and the control we have to retrain our brains.

+ We can then understand our body's response in reactions of fear or tension, and can learn how it is limiting access to our best state of mind. Noticing the responses, and what to do about it, can be life changing and allow us to see how we can be used for much more in the future.

What pray for the brain?

+ Based on our prayers accomplishing much (James 5:16, below in blue), praying for the brain allows us to target what we are asking for. This can greatly expand how we pray, and we can then pray for behavior related situations more specifically.

+ For example, praying for anxiety becomes more about praying for the brain functions that produce and remember fear. This allows us to notice our reactions more intently, and to bless another by praying for their brains. Or, rather than just medicating for a behavior, we can also pray for the healing of that brain and behavior.

"Therefore, confess your sins to one another, and pray for one another so that you may be healed. The effective prayer of a righteous man can accomplish much."
James 5:16

prayers for the brain?

So, these pages are for you whether:
- you have a minute, or
- you have an hour
  - you didn't even know you have an amygdala, or
  - you are neuroscientist
    - you are not even sure how to pray, or
    - you have prayed for years

For use in classes, small groups, retreats, book clubs ...

... in finally understanding your personal reactions, and how you relate to those around you ...

... as a resource for more reading and gift giving ideas.

... in teaching about the marvels of the brain ...

... in mentoring, counseling and therapy, for incorporating brain processing into behavioral healing ...

Day 1

A 30-day exploration.

Basic information on the brain structures and function.

Our Father Who Art in Heaven

I praise Your name for creating my

He

I

He
my
Help

Personalization:
a prayer
for your
brain,
based on the
format of the
Lord's Prayer.

Illustrations for learning locations and interactions of brain parts.

For Thine is the kingdom, and the power, and the glory forever and ever.
Amen!

Contemplation: a Bible verse for meditation.

of
NASB

More information and quotes.

"The Lord is my
whom shall I be afr

... each page

A Prayer for Another
To the Maker of the Amygdala, Prince of Peace*
*
As I learn how
and remem
I
[name of
Lord
is locked i
locked i
pr

Blessing:
a prayer for
someone else
and their healing
and growth,
with a
scripture reference*
for the Name of God

a ~ b ~ c
Three pages
for each
brain function,
increasing
your level of
knowledge.

amygdala

A big
reminder of a
brain function
that makes
you marvelous!

vii

welcome to the inside

amygdala
[ah-mig-doll-uh]

Two almond-shaped structures deep inside your brain in the "limbic system." These are your first reactors, sending chemicals throughout the rest of your brain. They also play an important role in fear response and setting memories in the brain. This system is part of the "fight, fright, flight" response.

anger
surprise
happiness
disgust
sadness
fear

Our Father Who Art in Heaven

I praise Your name for creating my
amygdala deep inside my brain.

Help me to understand more about it, so
that I can do more of Your will on this earth,
learning to use my emotional gatekeeper
for more joy than fear.

Forgive me for the reactions
I have that are from years of response,
for when I have been fearful
instead of looking first to You.
Help me to train my brain to notice when
my fearful reaction or anger is from habit.
Help me to see Your healing in my reactions.

For Thine is the kingdom, and the power,
and the glory forever and ever.
Amen!

your emotional gatekeeper

It makes the first reactions,
and has a memory of how to respond
(so my reaction might be just that).
You can retrain your brain to
have a different level of reaction.

amygdala

"The Lord is my light and my salvation.
whom shall I fear..." Psalm 27:1a NASB

# of your amazing brain!

A Prayer for Another
To the Maker of the Amygdala, Prince of Peace*

As I think about a mighty part of my brain created to be the emotional gatekeeper, and how it can remember previous responses, Lord, I think of _____ [name of family member, friend, co-worker].

I can see _____ locked in such fear and frantic reactions.

In Your name as the Prince of Peace, I pray for _____'s amygdala, that the alert level it stays at can be reduced.

Bless even their breathing, Oh Lord, so the release in tension can even be felt down their spinal cord and throughout their whole body.   Amen!   *Isaiah 9:6

amygdala

2

amygdala
[ah-mig-doll-uh]

They are involved in the processing of emotions, such as fear, anger and pleasure. How big the emotional response that is caused by an event determines what memories are stored, and where the memories are stored in the brain. A traumatic event can repeatedly cause a very startled response later, because the amygdala is still responding as if in the original event. Alert!

anger
surprise
disgust
sadness
fear
happiness

Our Father Who Art in Heaven,

I praise Your name for creating my amygdala to allow me to react to the world around me. Thank you that it can remember the joy I feel when I hear a friend laugh, or how afraid I felt when I heard a loved one was ill.

Help me to understand more about my inward parts, so that I can let my memories find their best place in my brain.

Forgive me for replaying bad memories in my mind, and having negative reactions over and over again, I can feel that my amygdala sends messages to release stress hormones through my brain at each trigger. Over and over and over again. Lord, be the healer of my amygdala.

For Thine is the kingdom, and the power, and the glory forever and ever. Amen!

mature at birth
and so children can have bigger joy and fear reactions from their amygdala, as the rest of the brain doesn't have experience enough to moderate the initial reactions.

"For I am the Lord your God, who upholds your right hand and says to you, do not fear. I will help you." Isaiah 41:13 NASB

amygdala

# of reactions

A Prayer for Another
To the King of Kings, Maker of the Amygdala*

As I learn how the amygdala is deep inside the brain,
and remembers how upsetting a situation was,
I think of _____
[name of family member, friend, co-worker].
Lord, I can see that _____
is locked in reacting to things that have happened;
locked in thinking that the remembering what
happened is protecting them from more pain,

Today, I intercede for
_____,
so that their amygdala can learn to
remember instead the comfort of
Your extended right hand.
You are there to rescue from thoughts
of fear, resentment and regret.

Thank you that You are
the King of healing. Amen!
*I Timothy 6:15

amygdala ~ b

amygdala

4

"low road" = react first

amygdala
[ah-mig-doll-uh]

They can react to an emotion with a "low road" which gets a message of say, fear, from the thalamus, and KABAM, the message goes to the spinal cord: FRIGHT, FLIGHT! Or a "high road," where the same trigger response goes instead to the prefrontal cortex and anterior cingulate to integrate information with reality. NO NEED TO RUN!

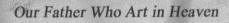

Corpus callosum (pages 25-30)

Cingulate gyrus (pages 19-24)

Hippocampus (pages 13-18)

Frontal lobe (pages 43-48)

Pre Frontal Cortex

Anterior Cingulate

Temporal lobe (pages 31-36)

Amygdala

Thalamus (pages 7-12)

Our Father Who Art in Heaven

I praise Your name for creating my amygdala,
to have a fast and slow switches.
Fast for when my body needs to respond
to get me out of danger, and slow
when I can use the rest of my brain
and memory to decide how fast I need to go!

Help me to understand more about it,
so that I can learn to realize when
I am being startled in fear and reacting,
and when I can use the other parts of my brain
to slow down my reactions.

Forgive me for often trusting my reactions more
than You, for getting energy from fight or flight,
when it may not be Christ-like at all.

For Thine is the kingdom, and the power,
and the glory, forever and ever. Amen!

"He restores my soul; He guides me in the paths of righteousness for His name's sake." Psalm 23:3 NASB

"we are all prisoners of it"

- Neuroscientist Joseph LeDoux, as [fear response] can be readily conditioned, but not so readily unconditioned.

"high road" = train your brain!

A Prayer for Another
To the Maker of the Amygdala, The Everlasting Father*

When I think of how You created a defense system in our brains, with a quick road and a slower road to reactions, I am thankful.

Yet Father, I think of _____
[name of family member, friend, co-worker].
I can clearly see now that their reactions are so automated for a quicker road of fear. _____ reacting so quickly, so impulsively, and so much damage is done.

Bless the healing of _____'s fear response path from the thalamus to the amygdala, and allow the paths to continue to the upper brain through the cingulate and to the frontal lobe.

Help _____ to feel the difference, and to know the healing peace that comes from their Everlasting Father.
Amen!

*Isaiah 9:6

amygdala
6

thalamus
[thal-uh-muhs]

This central part of the brain is a Greek word for courtyard or entrance room to a building, and acts as the relay station that sorts, processes and directs initial signals to the top of the rest of the brain, as well as down the spinal column.

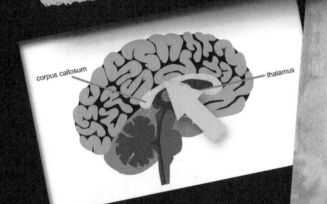

corpus callosum — thalamus

Our Father Who Art in Heaven

Thank you that as I enter Your courts with praise, You have created my thalamus on the top of my brain stem as the entrance station for all the senses in my brain.

Forgive me when I allow the processing to be a rush of overwhelming information, rather than a perfectly coordinated relay station, as You have designed it.

Lead me not into temptation to rely on substances to process what can seem so painful or overwhelming, but let Your perfect design work in me.

For Thine is the kingdom, and the power, and the glory forever and ever. Amen!

"Grand Central Station of sensory processing. Every sensation, mood, and thought passes through it as the information is relayed to other parts of the brain."
- Andrew Newberg and Mark Waldmon. How God Changes Things, page 54.

"Enter His gates with thanksgiving and His courts with praise! Give thanks to Him, bless His name."
Psalm 100:4 NASB

thalamus

7

A Prayer for Another
To the Rock of My Salvation,
Maker of the Thalamus*

As triggers come from seeing
something or hearing another thing,
I think of _____
[name of family member, friend, co-worker].
Allow their thalamas to send the
messages to the rest of the brain,
so that triggers are not the beginnings
of losing the ability to process the
flood of thoughts and feelings well.

Allow the connections in
_____'s
brain to fire in Your plan,
with the messages down the
spinal column to be that of
clear action, and not of panic
and fear. Be the Rock of
their Salvation and thalamus.
Amen!   *II Samuel 22:47

thalamus

thalamus [thal-uh-muhs]

As this deep internal organ brings information in from the senses, it's important function is in shifting attention. When you are reading a book, then you hear something and your focus shifts, that is your thalamus shifting and sorting the information coming in.

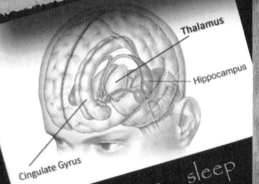

Thalamus

Hippocampus

Cingulate Gyrus

attention   sleep

arousal   wakefulness

Our Father Who Art in Heaven

You are the Creator of the command station that sits on top of my spinal column.

May Your kingdom be honored as my thalamus takes messages in and sends them to other parts of my brain.
May my thalamus be full of the best neuron firing responses to the rest of my brain.

As the messages send peace and calm throughout my body, forgive me for not letting that last. Instead, I often react from habits of fear and tension, when memories stored in my hippocampus play over and over. Help me to process each new situation well.

For Thine is the kingdom, and the power, and the glory forever. Amen!

"And with a pillar of cloud You led them by day, and with a pillar of fire by night to light for them the way in which they were to go."
Nehemiah 9:12 NASB

fire!

"The thalamic switching and integration mechanisms mean that when you encounter a fire, you see the flames, hear the crackling, and smell the smoke as a unified experience, which also includes remembering the taste of something burned and the pain of something hot."

- Frank Amthor, Neurology For Dummies, page 123.

thalamus

wagon wheel

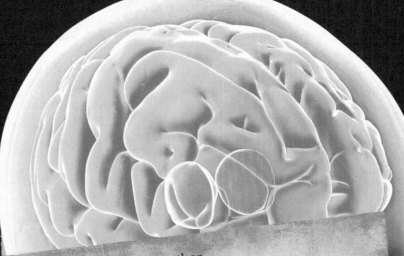

A Prayer for Another
To the Maker of the Thalamus, The Lord of Morning*

As the thalamus sends messages to other parts of the brain for processing, Lord, I know _____'s [name of family member, friend, coworker] brain has pathways with responses that are not what You intended. Reactions of low road to fright, flight and fight. As each new morning starts a new day, may this day be a new start for the reactions in _____'s brain.

May the connections to the frontal lobe system be healed for best decisions and future planning. May the neurons fire to the occipital lobe, so _____ can make a picture of what they would look like relying on You in their situation. Amen!   *II Samuel 23:4

thalamus

10

thalamus [thal-uh-muhs]

The pathway from the senses is much faster through the thalamus, than through other parts of the brain. Once a sound is registered by the thalamus in a rat, it only takes twelve milliseconds for the sound to travel to the amygdala. Then that amygdala sends chemical messages of how high you should jump...if you did see a rat!

Our Father Who Art in Heaven

When I learn about how fine-tuned you have created my brain, to protect me far faster than I can think, I worship Your name.

May I become so tuned in to You that my reactions become about responding as You would in every situation...in milliseconds.

Yet, I find my reactionary response is initially angry, or jumpy, or frightened. Please forgive me for not letting my thalamic system's signals be used for my best thinking, my best reactions.

Thank you for providing access to my frontal lobe sytems to help me make decisions today that reflect Your righteousness.

For Thine is the kingdom, and the power, and the glory forever and ever. Amen!

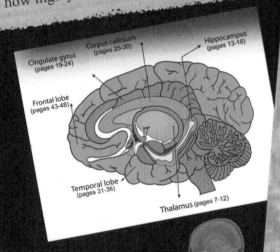

Cingulate gyrus (pages 19-24)
Corpus callosum (pages 26-30)
Hippocampus (pages 13-18)
Frontal lobe (pages 43-48)
Temporal lobe (pages 31-36)
Thalamus (pages 7-12)

quick and dirty

"The thalamic pathway is much quicker. It cannot tell the amygdala exactly what is there, but can provide a quick signal that warns that something dangerous may be there. Is it a quick and dirty processing system."

- Joseph LeDoux. The Emotional Brain, page 163.

"As for me, I shall behold Your face in righteousness; I will be satisfied with Your likeness when I awake."
Psalm 17:15 NASB

thalamus

marvels

thalamus

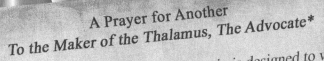

A Prayer for Another
To the Maker of the Thalamus, The Advocate*

It is so marvelous to know that my brain is designed to work in milliseconds to protect me. Today I think of _____'s [name of family member, friend, co-worker] thalamic pathways. Be the healer of messages processed to the amygdala, so the reactions of _____ are allowed to be from well-balanced systems of emotion in the limbic system and thought in the frontal lobes.

May the very many regions in the many regions in allow them to see connections coming from the thalamus to their brain allow for reactions and actions that more of You, to feel more of Your peace. Amen!   *I John 1:2

hippocampus

comes from the Greek word for "sea horse," because of its shape. Like the amygdala, it is in the limbic system. It is involved with the consolidation of short-term memories to long-term memories.

Our Father Who Art in Heaven

Thank you Lord for creating my hippocampus to be connected with other parts of my limbic system, so that even when I was very young I could learn and remember what was safe and what was dangerous.

Help me to be curious about how my memories have made me and my reactions...from delighted to terrified, from hesitant to remembering what worked well for me in the past.

Forgive me for often allowing my memories to connect like chains, each firing off each other, rather than allowing even my most painful memories to be captured and accepted. Let me feel the difference between the alert state of traumatic memories, and the peace that passes all understanding from You.

For Thine is the kingdom, and the power, and the glory forever and ever. Amen!

retrieving

long-term

memories

spacial

navigation

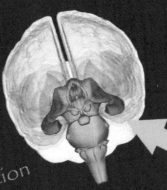

The Memory Store

"Memories are encoded in the neurons that created them. For example, sounds in the auditory cortex and emotions in the amygdala. The hippocampus pulls them together."

- Rita Carter, *The Human Brain Book*, page 199.

"Let all that I am praise the Lord; may I never forget the good things He does for me." Psalm 103:2 NLT

hippocampus

swimming in memories

A Prayer for Another
To the Maker of the Hippocampus, The Comforter*

As I think of how You created a memory system
in our brain, I am thankful.

Yet Father, I think of _____
[name of family member, friend, co-worker].
I can see clearly now that their memories control
their reactions before they have a chance to think.

Bless the healing of _____'s
hippocampus, so that memories can
become accepted as things that
happened, not threats that have
to be lived over and over again.

Help _____ to notice a shift
in how dominating a memory is,
and to feel vast changes in tension
and breathing as they get to know
You as their Comforter. Amen!
*Isaiah 9:6

hippocampus

14

hippocampus

Stress and trauma can cause difficulties in storing and retrieving memories. The memories can be deeply hidden, or can fire off constantly, keeping the whole body in a state of alert and danger.

This is because the very hormones used to send a body into action away from the threat, can keep the brain in a state of threat. Bodyguard gone wrong.

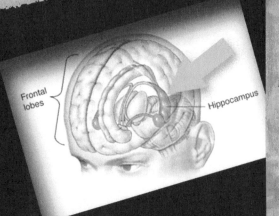

Frontal lobes — Hippocampus

Our Father Who Art in Heaven

I praise Your name for creating my hippocampus to be able to protect my mind from trauma, by allowing me to process my memories as I get older, and to know I don't have to keep re-living upsetting things.

Help me to be able to see the truth of even traumas in my memories, to be able to take responsbility for my continued responses of tension that I can feel in my whole body.

Forgive me for sometimes getting a negative energy from going over my memories, like a recording that won't stop. Help me to take a deep breath, and let my memories be just that: a memory, rather than a negative view that keeps control of me. Heal me, Oh Lord!

For Thine is the kingdom, and the power, and the glory forever and ever. Amen!

Stress Impact Zone

"...with prolonged stress irreversible changes take place. Cells in the hippocampus actually begin to degenerate. When this happens, the memory loss is permanent."

- Joseph LeDoux, *Emotional Brain*, page 242.

"When you go through deep waters. I will be with you. You will go through rivers of difficulty, you will not drown. When you go through the fires of oppression, you will not be burned up, and the flames will not consume you."

Isaiah 43:2 NLT

messes

A Prayer for Another
To the Maker of the Hippocampus, The Deliverer*

I am so thankful that my mind can retain memories of wonderful things that have happened. But Lord, I know _____ has [name of family member, friend, co-worker] had so many bad things happen in their life, even when they were very young.

Bless the healing of _____'s reaction to all the memories that continue to haunt and destroy their ability to see truth or delight in situations now. May the hormones produced in past dangers not be continually produced, keeping the danger level high. Let them feel a lessening of tension today.

Heal their hippocampus, so that even very difficult memories can be paths to You and seeing beyond the past pain. Let them know You are with them, and will be their Deliverer. Amen!   *Psalm 18:2

hippocampus ~ b

hippocampus

16

hippocampus

It plays back events and reactions, activating the frontal lobe system responses that were fired off in the original event itself.

This often happens in sleep, with the short-term memories in the hippocampus region of the brain. This playback process can be very damaged by stress, causing more stress.

long-term memory retrieval

spacial navigation

Hippocampus

Amygdala

Our Father Who Art in Heaven

You who created the hippocampus to replay memories, while checking in with other parts of the brain, I marvel at the design.

My memory replay, Lord, is often set off by triggers of sites, sounds and smells. I feel myself startled, and have trouble focusing on what is happening right now in my life. Forgive me for allowing that startled response to stop access to my best state of mind, which could see You as the strength in the situation.

Thank you that Your daily bread for me today is healing of that which has been damaged, those processes that are remembering from past pain.

For Thine is the kingdom, and the power, and the glory forever and ever. Amen!

Burned In The Brain

"Prolonged and severe stress damages the dendrite spines in the cells of the hippocampus, much like singeing the hair on your arm when you get too close to the fire....so they cannot repair themselves...The [recalled traumatic] memory is literally burned in [the] brain."
- Mary Holley. Crystal Meth, They Call It Ice, page 146.

hippocampus

"But the Helper, the Holy Spirit, whom the Father will send in my name, He will teach you all things, and bring to your remembrance all that I have said to you."
John 14:26 NASB

17

stuck on play

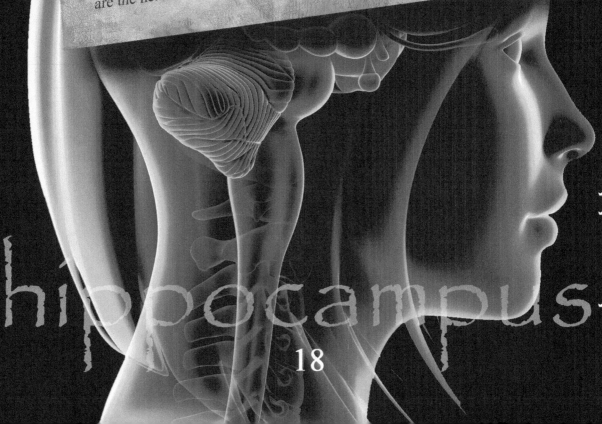

A Prayer for Another
To the Maker of the Hippocampus, The Commander*

I have so many memories that I love to let replay: happy memories.
Today I think of _____'s memory systems.
　　　　　　[name of family member, friend, co=worker]

There is such trouble between the hippocampus and the amygdala
in that brain, with memories all seared together, firing off, creating
such panic, anger and fear. Please be the separator of those memories.
Be the Commander of the movie theatre in _____'s head.

Bless their sleep, oh Lord. Let the processing of short-term and long-term
memories be as You designed it, to settle and not to startle. I believe You
are the healer of dendrites, cells, and neurons firing in all the right places.

*Isaiah 55:4

Amen!

hippocampus

cingulate [sing-gyuh-lit] gyrus [jayh-ruhs]

lies between the top of the brain (frontal, parietal and occipital cortexes), and the middle of the brain (limbic system).

It is one of the balancers in the brain between thinking and emotional reactivity.

It's functions include resolution of conflicts, goal setting, and compassion.

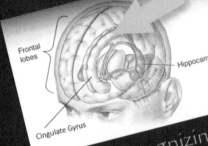

Frontal lobes

Hippocampus

Cingulate Gyrus

empathy

recognizing errors

self-awareness

Our Father Who Art in Heaven

Just as You created the heavens above
and the earth below, I praise You for creating
the cingulate to wrap around my corpus
callosum and lower limbic system,
creating pathways between the top
and bottom of my brain.

When I am overthinking a situation,
or over reacting, forgive for not allowing
this part of me to balance,
and see You at work in my situation.

Help me to even feel when the clarity comes,
when my cingulate tells the rest of my brain
that a resolution has been reached, and I breathe.

For Thine is the kingdom, and the power,
and the glory forever and ever. Amen!

The Personal Assistant

"If the prefrontal cortex is the board chairman, the cingulate gyrus is the personal assistant… provides the chairman with certain filtering information and assists in teleconferencing with other parts of the brain, especially the amygdala, which helps create and maintain emotions." - John Medina, Brain Rules, page 80.

"But the goal of our instruction is love from a pure heart and a good conscience and a sincere faith."
I Timothy 1:5 NASB

19

bottom up

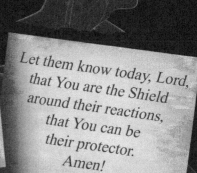

A Prayer for Another
To Tne Creator of my Cingulate Gyrus,
My Shield Around Me*

I marvel at the part of my brain that wraps like a shield over the top of my limbic emotional system, providing connections to the top of my brain.

_____
[name of family member, friend, co-worker]
has been through so much trauma that their connections through their cingulate gyrus have not developed well, and thoughts can not be stopped, or they seemingly can't avoid conflicts.

Let them know today, Lord, that You are the Shield around their reactions, that You can be their protector.
Amen!

*Psalm 3:3

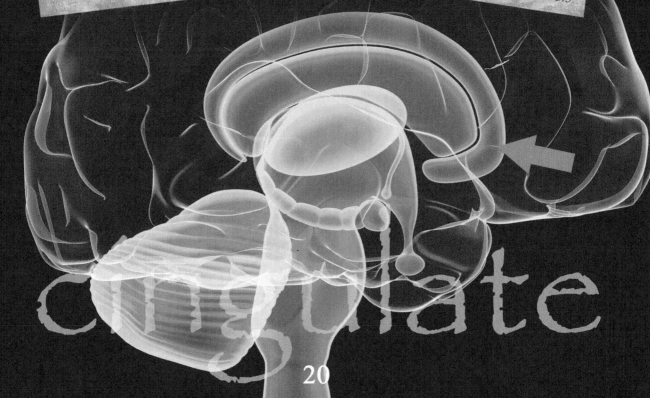

cingulate

20

fully

cingulate [sing-gyuh-lit]
gyrus [jayh-ruhs]

This area is loaded with spindle cells, which respond extremely quickly, and as humans we have a thousand times more than other species. The spindles are four times longer than other neurons, and are thought to allow for faster transmission, including snap judgments.

Our Father Who Art in Heaven

I honor Your name for creating specific neurons for different jobs in my brain, with changes in shape and sizes.

Forgive me for using my spindle cells for faster processing without wisdom, for making snap decisions and judgments that don't line up with Your will.

Thank you for providing in this day the ability to show empathy and compassion that model Yours, rather than my initial responses that definitely are not like You.

For Thine is the kingdom, and the power, and the glory forever and ever. Amen!

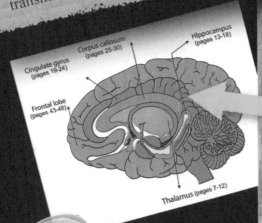

Cingulate gyrus (pages 19-24)
Corpus callosum (pages 25-30)
Hippocampus (pages 13-18)
Frontal lobe (pages 43-48)
Thalamus (pages 7-12)

the social brain

"The location of spindle cells and their connection of the regions of the social brain illustrate their importance in social relatedness, [and] ...emotion. Spindle cells have rich synaptic receptors for dopamine, serotonin, and vasopressin, which play a role in mood and thus in our emotional experiences and bonding. They form connections between the cingulate cortex and the frontal cortex."
- John B. Arden, *Rewire Your Brain*, page 13.

cingulate gyrus

"He has made His wonders to be remembered. The Lord is gracious and compassionate."
Psalm 111:4 NASB

A Prayer for Another
To the Creator of my Cingulate, Lifter of My Head*

It is fascinating to think that my empathy for others comes
from so many specifically created neurons that
fire together to make judgments and provide insight.
I think of _____'s
[name of family member, friend, co-worker]
impulsivity that causes this same system to fire differently,
so they act without empathy or compassion.

Continue to heal the front (anterior) of their cingulate cortex,
so that they are able to bond and connect with others
that You have put in their path (like me).
Amen!   *Psalm 3:3

cingulate

cingulate [sing-gyuh-lit]
gyrus [jayh-ruhs]

The balancing regions is known by researchers in the past decade to be impacted by meditation, especially the front, or anterior cingulate. Brain scans show increased neural activity in this area, especially after twelve minutes in practiced meditators. This makes sense: focusing on our Creator, and letting thoughts of Him replace fear, tension, and over thinking. Thoughts of planning, compassion and empathy then fill our minds.

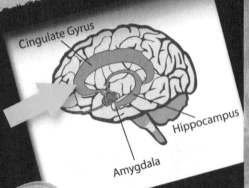

Cingulate Gyrus

Hippocampus

Amygdala

Our Father Who Art in Heaven

Your presence in the temple of my mind is what I seek and long for while I am on the earth.

Please forgive me when flooding emotions in my limbic system, and frantic thoughts of planning keep me from being able to focus on You. Help me to notice when I can't even sit still in Your presence.

Thank you for giving me instead the flood of peace and joy when I meditate on Your word, and then am able to be still in my mind to hear from You. Thank you for the cingulate's involvement in this process, acting as the balancer between my thoughts and my emotions.

For Thine is the kingdom, and the power, and the glory forever and ever. Amen!

cingulate gyrus

"One thing I have asked from the Lord that I shall seek; that I may dwell in the house of the Lord all the days of my life, to behold the beauty of the Lord, and to meditate in His temple."
Psalm 27:4 NASB

to-ing & fro-ing

"The anterior [front] cingulate cortex also seems to be activated during mind-fullness meditation... takes as the focus of its reflective practice two subjects: breathing and the changing to-ing and fro-ing of the mind from thought to thought, feeling to feeling." – John B. Arden and Lloyd Linford, *Brain-Based Therapy*, page 251.

meditation

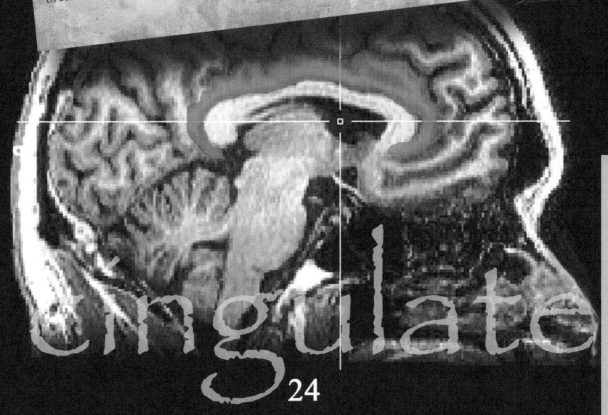

A Prayer for Another
To the Creator of my Cingulate, the Rest of My Soul*

Today I intercede for _____
[name of family member, friend, co-worker],
who is experiencing all the visceral response of a racing mind and
flooded emotions. _____ can't sort through the
panic in the flood of tension enough to take time to go to You as the rest
for their soul, the One who can calm the racing thoughts and floods.

Fill _____ with feelings of great peace that helps them to
breathe well, so their cingulate can get marvelous new oxygen. Amen!

*Psalm 23:3

cingulate

24

corpus callosum [cal·lo·sum]

Latin for "tough body,"
which connects the left and right hemispheres
with a thick fiber tract (200 million fibers).
We used to think of "left" and "right" brain thinkers.
Now we focus more on the
two hemispheres working together,
using the left to process details,
and the right for looking at the bigger picture.

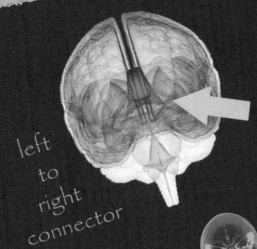

left
to
right
connector

Our Father Who Art in Heaven

I marvel at You who created this band of millions
of fibers connecting so much of my brain.

Understanding Your will in my life is all about
a balance of noticing details, and yet looking
around for the bigger picture. Help me look.

Please give me more awareness of old
habits of thinking, and help me work to use
different thinking systems in my mind.
Forgive me for relying on how I have thought
in the past, and expecting others to do
as they have done in the past.

Help me to see Your creativity all around me, as
I become more connected in my corpus callosum,
and to access more of it for blessing others.

For Thine is the kingdom, and the power,
and the glory forever and ever. Amen!

long distance connections

"It serves to connect distant neurons
that fire together, adding dimension
and depth to everything you do and
think."

- John B. Arden, *Rewire Your Brain*, page 3.

corpus callosum

"The Lord is my light and my salvation.
of whom shall I be afraid....."
Psalm 27:1a NASB

25

righty

A Prayer for Another Maker of the Corpus Callosum, The Almighty*

It is amazing to think You have created us to have two separate sides of our brains, that work best when connected.
But Lord, I know _____
[name of family member, friend, co-worker] gets stuck on the small picture and is not able to see the bigger picture of what You are doing in their life,
as Almighty over all messes.

Bless the left and right of them Lord, the very neurons working in the fibrous connections of the brain.
Let them feel a release in tension as they look to You as the creator of their whole brain.

Add dimension and depth in their life, even as they feel so disconnected.
Let _____ know You are the Almighty! Amen!
*Revelation 1:8

corpus callosum

26

corpus callosum [cal·lo·sum]

in a female is denser, thus the two sides of the
brain work more evenly. This causes a better
connection to the lower part of the brain:
more emotional connections (limbic system)
with words (temporal lobe)
having more emotional content.
Men tend to use the side of the brain needed
for the task at hand.

Our Father Who Art in Heaven

It is fascinating, Lord, that in the image of
You, two brains were created that are so different.
Thank you that that design plan is a way of
meeting our needs, providing our daily bread.

Forgive me for not using my best brain design
to function at its best, either male or female.

Help me to learn to be more connected:
to either finish tasks before me,
or feel more of what is happening around me.
Thank you for creating this marvelous
corpus callosum to provide roads of responses
throughout my whole brain.

**For Thine is the kingdom, and the power,
and the glory forever and ever. Amen!**

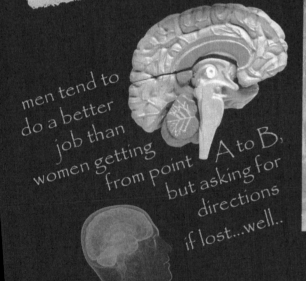

men tend to
do a better
job than
women getting
from point A to B,
but asking for
directions
if lost...well..

Road Construction

"Picture ... a map showing the areas for
emotions in the brains of the two sexes.
In the man's brain, the connecting routes
between the area would be country roads
and in the woman's brain, they would
be super highways ... "
- Louann Brizendine, Female Brain, page 127.

corpus callosum

"God created man in His own image,
in the image of God He created him;
male and female He created them."
Genesis 1:27 NASB

and freeways

A Prayer for Another
To the Maker of the Corpus Callosum, My Fortress*

Thank you Lord for the different thinking processes
in men and women. But Lord, I know _____
[name of family member, friend, co-worker]
is not balanced between top brain thinking,
and middle brain emotional processing.
There have been too many wounds over time,
not allowing their reactions to land safely.

Connect roads of their thinking
for them, Lord.
Slow down that fast freeway
thinking, and help that
country road mind to find
the best way to think and feel.

Heal their corpus callosum.
Please protect and
defend _____'s
brain, as their Fortress!
Amen!

*Psalm 18:2

corpus callosum-b

corpus callosum

corpus callosum [cal.lo.sum]

This is the area of the brain that can cause limited ability to relate to those around, especially learning how to relate socially. Do you remember the movie "Rain Man" in 1988? Dustin Hoffman's role was a first introduction to autism for many of us. Autism, and its related spectrum of behavior, often limit many areas of thinking, and cause an advanced ability in others. Haven't seen the movie? Hoffman dedicated himself to honoring those with reduced nerve fibers.

Our Father Who Art in Heaven

Lord, as I look around and see someone, even in my own house, that does not have the neuro connections in their corpus collosum for relating, it seems hard to see the plan of Your perfect will.

Thank you for providing the energy every day for understanding the mind of one who struggles, one who doesn't fit in, one who is not understood.

I look to You to help me believe we are all fearfully and wonderfully made, and created in the image of You, though it is often far beyond my understanding.

For Thine is the kingdom, and the power, and the glory forever and ever. Amen!

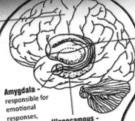

Cerebral cortex - a thin layer of gray matter on the surface of the cerebral hemispheres. Two-thirds of its area is deep in the tissues or folds. Responsible for the higher mental functions, general movement, perception, and behavioral reactions. (Frontal Cortex Pages 43-48)

Amygdala - responsible for emotional responses, including aggressive behavior. (Pages 1-6)

Hippocampus - makes it possible to remember new information and recent events. (Pages 13-18)

Basal ganglia - gray masses deep in the cerebral hemisphere that serves as a connection between the cerebrum and cerebellum. Helps to regulate automatic movements.

Major Brain Structures Implicated in Autism

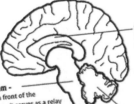

Brain stem - located in front of the cerebellum, it serves as a relay station, passing messages between various parts of the body and the cerebral cortex. Primitive functions essential to survival (breathing and heart rate control) are located here. (Pages 49-54)

Corpus callosum - consists primarily of closely packed bundles of fibers that connect the right and left hemisphere and allows for communication between the hemispheres. (Pages 25-30)

Cerebellum - located at the back of the brain, it fine tunes our motor activity, regulates balance, body movements, coordination, and the muscles used in speaking.

the voice that couldn't speak

"I am much less autistic now, compared to when I was young. I remember some behaviors like picking carpet fuzz and watching spinning plates for hours. I didn't want to be touched. I couldn't shut out background noise. I didn't talk until I was about 4 years old. I screamed. I hummed. But as I grew up, I improved."
- Temple Grandin, author and autistic activist

Hi Ben!

repetitive and restricted behaviors

"I will give thanks to You, for I am fearfully and wonderfully made; wonderful are Your works, and my soul knows it very well."
Psalm 139:13-15 NLT

corpus callosum

unexpected routes

Fiber tracts coming from the corpus callosum providing inter hemispheric linkage between specific cortical regions. Imagine less of these...

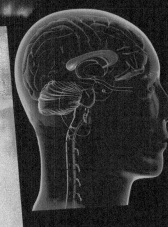

A Prayer for Another
To the Maker of the Corpus Callosum, My High Tower*

I know how often I feel overwhelmed in life, relating to people, keeping up with to do lists and schedules. Lord, I know

_____
[name of family member, friend, co-worker]

has a brain that doesn't have all the connective fibers, or is parenting a child with autism related behaviors.

Thank you for being the high tower, a source of strength in these situations. Thank you for providing the understanding needed to relate to others, or to parent one who can't communicate.

I pray for healing of connectors in the corpus callosum in _____'s. brain. Amen!   *Psalm 18:2

hear no evil

temporal lobe

located behind the ears, stretching from the front to the back. Memory functions of words are processed in the left side, and word tones on the right side.
Also processes rhythm and music.
The top of these lobes gets the brain ready for the next breath.

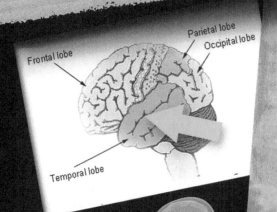

Frontal lobe
Parietal lobe
Occipital lobe
Temporal lobe

memory
language
mood stability
facial recognition

temporal lobe

"Hear my prayer, O God;
Give ear to the words of my mouth."
Psalm 54:2 NASB

Our Father Who Art in Heaven

To hear Your name and to speak Your name is a gift that I often take for granted.

In this brain part that stretches along the outside of my brain, and does such important processing connecting with the inside, I seek to hear from You, so that I might do Your will while I live on this earth.

My words are often quick and harsh. I don't take time to let my brain balance when I hear things. I am often so angry I miss the expression on someone else's face. Forgive me for not letting my temporal lobes work well.

Please protect me from hearing evil things.

For Thine is the kingdom, and the power, and the glory forever and ever. Amen!

Complicated Chit Chat

"Conversation comes naturally to most of us, but in terms of brain function it is one of the most complicated cerebal activities we can engage in."
- Rita Carter. Human Brain Book, page 148.

speak no evil

A Prayer for Another
To My Sanctuary,
Maker of the Temporal Lobes*

As I think of conversations,
_____ comes to my mind
[name of family member, friend, co-worker].
Their words are so cutting and harsh,
and they don't seem to be impacted
by the responses on another's face.
Allow for healing in their temporal
lobes, both on the left and right sides,
so they can hear another's kindness.

Thank you for bringing
_____
a special song somewhere today,
something to remind them
that You are their Sanctuary.
Let them feel Your safety
and peace.   Amen!
* Isaiah 8:14

temporal lobe

temporal lobe

manages anger, fear, frustration and depression. Also involved in epilepsy and schizophrenia (people hearing voices and having imaginary conversations). Remember John Nash in the movie "A Beautiful Mind"? In contrast, when this area of the brain is balanced, it can provide a positive spiritual experiences.

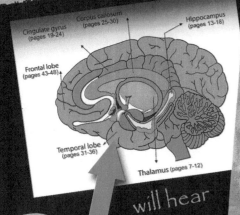

Cingulate gyrus (pages 19-24)
Corpus callosum (pages 25-30)
Hippocampus (pages 13-18)
Frontal lobe (pages 43-48)
Temporal lobe (pages 31-36)
Thalamus (pages 7-12)

will hear someone as critical when they are not

Our Father Who Art in Heaven

Thank you for creating regions around my ears, so that I might speak and hear Your name.

Forgive me for loosing my compassion, when my reaction to someone's anger is to feel as though I am always walking on egg shells. I feel jumpy, and I am afraid. Remind me of all the connections from different regions of the brain to the temporal lobes, and how there may have been damage causing the angry, unpredictable responses.

Your grace is sufficient in this situation, so thank you for allowing me to act as You would. Allow me to speak with words from You.

For Thine is the kingdom, and the power, and the glory forever and ever. Amen!

Robbers In House

"We may have a very angry person... perhaps, someone who rages inappropriately and is easily set off. Someone who makes others feel as though they always have to walk on egg shells in order to avoid triggering their explosive temper... As you can imagine, anger is one of life's most common joy robbers." — Earl Henslin. This Is Your Brain On Joy, page 27.

temporal lobe

"Whatever you do in word or deed, do all in the name of the Lord Jesus, giving thanks through Him to God the Father." Colossians 3:17 NASB

the egg shells

A Prayer for Another
To the Creator of my Frontal Lobes, The Great Light*

As I think about explosive anger and eggshells,
it does not take long for _____ to come to mind.
[name of family member, friend, co-worker], I intercede today for
their temporal lobes, for healing in what has been damaged.
May the words spoken to them today enter the very complex
system for hearing, including comparing the new words with
past words. Allow them to hear the new. Shed your great light on
them today, so they notice the state of tension they live in.
Then let them hear the comfort of Your voice.
Amen!   *Isaiah 9:2

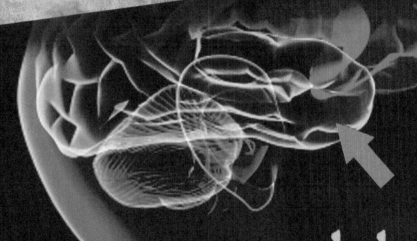

temporal lobe

temporal lobe

The inside, or medial portion, lies next to the limbic system (about the size of a walnut). This partnership allows us to accurately determine another's emotional state. The healthy system has good memory control, and word retrieval. Then relationships are positive.

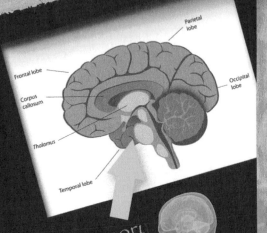

memory
language
mood stability
facial recognition

temporal lobe

Our Father Who Art in Heaven

The design of my brain, where regions
meet and interact, allows me to be reminded
of the amazing design. Thank you for
the limbic system next to the inside of the
temporal lobe. May my memories and
reactions be honoring to You, so that
I can be part of Your will in my actions.

Yet, I hear things and I feel the reactions of tension
on my breathing and throughout my body.
My amygdala is still yelling "alert,"
and that is all I can hear. Be the healer of
what I hear from the inside, and outside!

Allow me to retrieve the words in my temporal
lobes that I have learned about You,
Bible verses that I have memorized.

**For Thine is the kingdom, and the power,
and the glory forever and ever. Amen!**

Even Keeled...Not!

"When there are problems in these parts
of the brain, our memories suffer, we
either lack spiritual experience or have
destructive ones, and experience mood
swings and a temper out of control."
- D. Amen, *Healing Hardware of the Soul*, page 62.

"Even before there is a word on my tongue,
Behold, O Lord, You know it all."
Psalm 139:4 NASB

wonders

A Prayer for Another
To My Rock of Ages*, Creator of my Temporal Lobe

As messages come into the thalamus from the ears, Lord please sharpen the connection that is sent to the limbic system and to the temporal lobe in _____.
[name of family member, friend, co-worker],
Allow their amygdala and hippocampus in the limbic system to heal, so that _____s responses to situations are not from anger and reaction to old memories.
Let the neural connections in the frontal lobe system allow the temporal lobes to have balanced reactions of mood stability, instead of firecracker like reactions.
Amen!   *Isaiah 9:2

temporal lobe

temporal lobe ~ c

do you see

occipital lobe [oc·cip·i·tal]

Most of the messages from the retina in the eye go to the thalamus, and are sent to the occipital lobe. From there different parts of the brain process the information (see next pages), and then it goes to the frontal lobes. This allows you to figure out what you are seeing, and how to react to it.

Our Father Who Art in Heaven

Your are the Creator of the concept
of millions, that I can hardly comprehend,
let alone that of millions and millions.

Continue to heal the pathway between
my retina in my eyes, to my thalamus, to
the explosion of neurons in my occipital lobe.
Allow me, Oh Lord, to see Your eternal work
more clearly, through all that I see on this earth.

Forgive me when those paths are clogged
and blocked by memories from the past,
adding danger messages from my limbic system
to what I see. Allow me to slow down
enough to breathe well, and see You instead.

For Thine is the kingdom, and the power,
and the glory, forever and ever. Amen!

Parietal lobe
Occipital lobe
Frontal lobe
Temporal lobe

light
dark
motion
speed

occipital

"O taste and see that the Lord is good;
how blessed is the man
who takes refuge in Him!"
Psalm 34:8 NASB

million schmillion

"A little over one million retinal ganglian cells project to about the same number of... cells in the thalamus. However, each thalamic relay neuron projects to over 100 visual area neurons... Understanding the immensely complex visual processing network that takes up nearly half of all the neocortex is one of the most challenging areas of research in neuroscience today."
- Frank Amthor. Neuroscience for Dummies, page 96.

what I see?

A Prayer for Another
To The Strength for The Needy,
Maker of the Occipital Lobe*

I am amazed to think about
how much of my vision is at
work when I don't even realize it.
Today, I lift up _____
[name of family member, friend, co-worker].
The pathways of their vision have
been rewired to explosive responses,
and they can no longer see clearly.
They are blinded to who You are.

You are the strength for the needy,
and I believe that is even for the
millions of neurons in their
occipital lobes.
May You be the strength in
those connections, so _____
can see Your care for them. Amen!

* Isaiah 25:4

occipital

occipital lobe [oc·cip·i·tal]

After passing through the occipital region, the messages go up (dorsal route - the "where") to determine position, movement, size, and shape. The information also leaves occipital region down (ventral route - the "what") to the inside of the temporal lobe, adding meaning. Then off to the frontal lobes for conscious perception of what was seen.

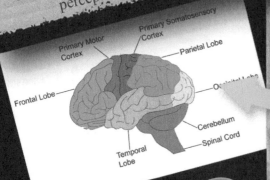

size

shape

movement

position

Our Father Who Art in Heaven

As I understand more about how complex my vision system is, I marvel at You.

I go so quickly through my day to day life that I miss so much of the beauty You have placed in my life for me to see. Thank you for all the parts of my brain at work when I see things that are so familiar to me, and things that are new.

Continue to heal me, so that even when life is overwhelming to me, I can stop and use the beauty around me to use different parts of my brain. Forgive me for not stopping to look at the rose, and the sunset. Help me to lift up my eyes when I am feeling paralyzed.

For Thine is the kingdom, and the power, and the glory, forever and ever. Amen!

quick! duck!

"The dorsal, or "where" path ... gathers information about motion and timing that is integrated into the action plan. All the information needed to, say, duck [from] a flying object, is gathered along this path with no need for conscious thought."
- Rita Carter, *The Human Brain Book*, page 82.

"I will lift up my eyes to the mountains; from where shall my help come? My help comes from the Lord, who made heaven and earth."
Psalm 121:1-2 NASB

occipital

A Prayer for Another
To the Creator of my Occipital Lobes,
My Foundation*
_____

As I begin to pray, I can clearly see _____
[name of family member, friend, co-worker],
locked in the paralysis of fear from the past.
Today, please give them things of beauty to see that cause
them to lift their eyes up, to allow the oxygen to flow
freely, away from being used primarily in their brain stem
(working so hard to keep just their major organs alive).

Allow them to blink and see clearly in front of them, so
their thalamus, occciptal lobe, and limbic system can
react from messages of balance from their frontal lobes.
Let the millions of neurons clearly see how
You are at work as their Foundation.   Amen!

*Isaiah 28:6

occipital

40

occipital lobe [oc·cip·i·tal]

The information also leaves this region and heads down (ventral route) to the inside of the temporal lobe to find the "what," and checks out memories related to the object or event. The amygdala says "one of my favorite faces!," and then up to the frontal lobe for a final party to figure out what was seen in a conscious manner.

Frontal lobe
Corpus callosum
Thalamus
Temporal lobe
Parietal lobe
Occipital lobe

joy-booster!

"Visual prayer is a way of connecting several joy-boosting practices at once: contemplating a scene of beauty while relaxing and praying for your own well-being or that of someone else's is a marvelous way to be a more joyful person.

face
recognition
shape
color

"Let your eyes look directly ahead and let your gaze be fixed straight in front of you. Watch the path of your feet, and all your ways will be established."
Prov 4:25-26 NASB

Our Father Who Art in Heaven

As I think about sight and my earthly brain, I realize have no capacity to see and behold a picture of You in Your glory.

Thank you that on this earth, You have given me millions of neurons to see, perceive, and act. May my actions be part of Your kingdom plan on this earth, including accepting things that I do not understand. Allow me to see the picture of what I would look like in that acceptance (the situation simply is, and I have the strength to deal with it).

Show me what I would look like if I acted with the mind of Christ.

Amen!

"Perhaps this is why the Twenty-third Psalm is so popular. It is one of the most visual, relaxing, and joyful prayers in the Bible, and its picture of God's shepherding nearness - even through the dark valleys - is immensely comforting to anxious spirits."

- Earl Henslin, *This Is Your Brain On Joy*, page 53.

prayer

A Prayer for Another
To the Maker of my Occipital Lobe, My Hiding Place*

I am praying today that You will be _____ 's
[name of family member, friend, co-worker] Hiding Place.
That You will grant them the picture of You shepherding
them to calm and quiet waters, so their soul can rest in You.
Bring pictures to their mind of beautiful places they have
seen, and let them experience the chemical changes that
come even in a good memory. Let this visual process allow
the oxygen to move, the synapses to fire in their neurons,
so that the danger levels can decrease.

Help them come to acceptance for what You are
doing in their lives, and in their families.
Let them feel the peace of You, as their limbic
system reacts   with joy, instead of trauma.
                        Amen!   *Isaiah32:2

occipital

occipital ~ c

frontal lobes

They sit in your forehead, above and behind your eyes. The front part processes emotions into complex feelings. The frontal lobes help us anticipate the actions of other people. They check in with the limbic system to weigh out risks and dangers, planning and setting goals.

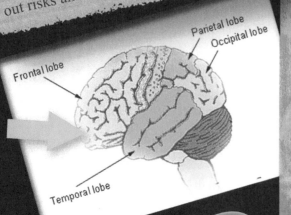

Parietal lobe
Occipital lobe
Frontal lobe
Temporal lobe

anticipation
planning

frontal lobes

Our Father Who Art in Heaven

May Your name be praised for being
the ultimate in planners, as You are aware
of all that goes on in a sense of time
that I can hardly begin to understand.

You have given me the ability to plan, to
set goals, and to anticipate what is coming
ahead. Thank you for this ability, and
how it is a part of Your great provision for me.

And somehow I continue to fear and fret
for my future, not allowing my frontal brain
to plan well, to have excellent judgment in
the very complex situations I find myself in.

As my frontal lobes help in evaluating what I see
with my eyes, may I clearly see You at work.

For Thine is the kingdom, and the power,
and the glory forever and ever. Amen!

Mack truck in the mirror

"The frontal and prefrontal areas work together to solve problems, like what to do when a truck appears in your rear-view mirror going twenty miles per hour faster than you. Fear and logical thinking work together to get out of the way in time."
– Mary Holley, *Crystal Meth, They Call It Ice*, page 23.

"Trust in the Lord with all your heart,
and do not lean on your own understanding.
In all your ways acknowledge Him,
and He will make your paths straight."
Proverbs 3:5, 6 NASB

43

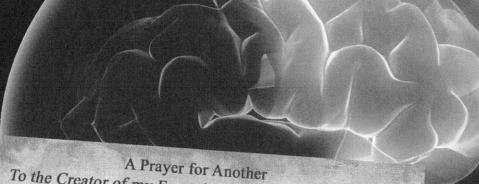

fantastic deliberations

A Prayer for Another
To the Creator of my Frontal Lobes, My Strong Rock*

Thank you for this part of my brain that uses information from other parts of my brain, and then makes judgements and decisions. Today, I look at the decision making pattern of _____
[name of family member, friend, co-worker]
and it is apparent that their frontal lobes are not working as well as You intended when You created them.

Allow them to be aware of their emotional reactions in their limbic system, and their habits of thinking, that keep them in cycles of decision making that is so harmful to themselves and others around them. Just as a strong rock is a very steady foundation, be their Strong Rock for the very foundation of their thinking.
Amen! *Psalm 31:2

frontal lobes

44

frontal lobes

This front part of the brain houses the ability to see results of current actions, and choose between good and bad activities. Impulsivity is monitored, and in a healthy brain, stops us from saying and doing things that cause harm to ourselves or others around us. In adults this area reaches maturity after the 20s.

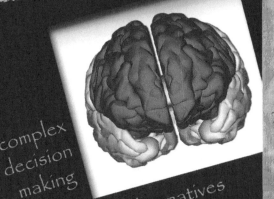

complex decision making

weighing of alternatives
short term reward
long term consequence

frontal lobes

"So, as those who have been chosen of God, holy and beloved, put on a heart of compassion, kindness, humility, gentleness and patience; bearing with one another, and forgiving each other, whoever has a complaint against anyone; just as the Lord forgave you, so also should you."
Colossians 3:12-13 NASB

Our Father Who Art in Heaven

In this part of my brain that is able to anticipate the results of my actions, I anticipate being able to see Your name glorified through me.

Thank you for all the connections between my frontal lobes and my physical body, which protect me from impulsive responses in my initial reactions to surprises and stresses.

Help me to be more forgiving of those around me with impulsivity issues: someone who speaks too quickly, or acts before they think. Grant me a curiosity about their brain formation, and let me be a part of what You are doing in them.

Thank You for my frontal lobes allowing me to look into the future, and see Your grace covering me.

For Thine is the kingdom, and the power, and the glory forever and ever. Amen!

The Moral Center

"...plays a leading role in character and moral development. It also allows us to see beyond ourselves and enables us to empathize with others. It allows us to anticipate the future so that we can appreciate the consequences of our actions, and be socially responsible"
- Daniel Amen. Hardware of the Soul, page 86.

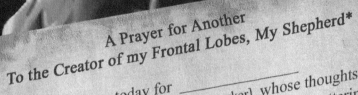

A Prayer for Another
To the Creator of my Frontal Lobes, My Shepherd*

I pray today for _____
[name of family member, friend, co-worker], whose thoughts
and actions seem to be so impulsive, as sheep scattering
in a field. It seems as if there is not a chance for the thoughts
to be gathered and considered. The neurons firing between all
different areas of their brains are just not connecting well.
Be their Shepherd, Lord, even in the gathering of their impulses.

Let them feel their initial reactions as a burst of tension.
Allow them to breathe, and pause for just a moment,
so their frontal lobes can heal to be a center of keen judgment.
Amen!   *Psalm 23:3

frontal lobes

frontal lobes

They are the center for wisdom and flexibility, allowing us to adjust quickly, to change plans in seconds if in danger. But, trauma over time greatly impacts this thinking process. This processing causes conditions such as post traumatic stress disorder (PTSD), attention deficit disorders (ADHD), substance abuse, and other disorders.

Our Father Who Art in Heaven

Holy is Your name, especially as I consider this center of wisdom in my brain.

Events from my past, things that were done to me, things that people said, are quite a mess in my reactions. Forgive me for the series of thoughts, like run away trains, that feel like they will destroy me. Help me to see the picture of me, as You do. Let me see that picture, so the trains stop.

Amen!

stone rolling down hill

"The structural changes   in the brain resulting from childhood trauma weaken the connections between the higher cortical areas and the emotional limbic areas, so emotions are harder to conrol. The imbalance between cortical (reasoning) and limbic (feeling) brain function leads to uncontrolled thought processes (obsessions), and disruptive memories (flashbacks)."

dissaciation
PTSD
ADHD
OCD

frontal lobes

"The steps of a man are established by the Lord,
And He delights in his way.
When he falls, he will not be hurled headlong,
because the Lord is the One who holds his hand."
Psalm 37:23-24 NASB

"Obsessive thoughts and feelings of worthlessness, ugliness, rejection, and humiliation require a conscious effort to 'stop thinking like that.' As soon as the reasoning cortex lets up the command to 'stop thinking like that' (around 2 o'clock in the morning) the limbic circuits revert to their old pattern of obsessive thoughts and compulsive behaviors."
- M. Holley, *Crystal Meth*, page 147.

of the drama

A Prayer for Another
To the Maker of the Frontal Lobes,
The Everlasting God*

When considering the impact of trauma on the brain,
it does not take long for me to consider
_____
[name of family member, friend, co-worker].
They were just precious children when terrible
things happened in their home, or they turned to
substances, or the tension in their homes now
continues to keep the chaos in their thinking process.

I know that Your love for _____ is
everlasting, and You can heal the connections
between their thalamus, amygdala, hippocampus,
and frontal lobe centers. Allow the nerves
to their outside body feel a great release in tension
today, so that the obsessive thoughts have no value.
Let them see the picture You have for them as
being of high value, with a great purpose.

Bless even their blinking and breathing today,
so that vital chemicals can allow clarity of thought.
Be the Everlasting Conductor of their trains!
Amen!   *Isaiah 40:28

frontal lobes

frontal lobes ~ c

brain stem

A vital structure of the brain that serves many functions while connecting to the spinal column and the rest of the body. The nerve connections that run the body, and the sensory systems that allow us to feel all those connections, happen in the brain stem.

It is the center of many automatic functions such as eating, sleeping, heart rate and breathing.

Our Father Who Art in Heaven

Your name be praised for creating the connection between my brain and my body, to keep so much of me functioning automatically.

May my understanding of this marvelous connection help me to understand what I can and cannot control about me, as Your will is done around me.

Forgive me for not caring for this body of mine, so all that functions on its own has to work so much harder. My heart. My lungs. My stomach. Deliver me from the evils of substances.

For Thine is the kingdom, and the power, and the glory forever and ever. Amen!

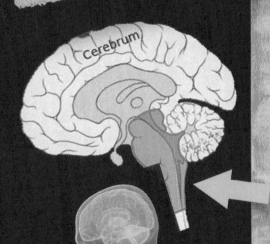

Cerebrum

permanent injury

After injury, damage to the brain stem may be permanent, as the nerves in the brain stem do not regenerate. More reason to pray!
See pages 55-60 for more information on breathing.

"Then the Lord God formed man of dust from the ground, and breathed into his nostrils the breath of life; and man became a living thing."
Genesis 2:6 NASB

brain stem

must go down

A Prayer for Another
To the Maker of the Brain Stem, The Mighty God*

Thinking about this mighty channel of nerve fibers between the top and bottom of me, Lord I think of _____ [name of family member, friend, co-worker] whose automatic body functions aren't working well. With the emotional center of the limbic system right smack dab on top of the brain stem, the automatic systems are worn out. _____'s heart isn't beating in a healthy, regular rhythm, or there is seemingly permanent damage to their spinal cord system.

I look to You as Mighty God in this physical situation, and ask You to intervene for healing. Amen! *Isaiah 9:6

brain stem

and now I lay me down

brain stem

The medulla oblongata is one of the parts of the brain stem that processes information about many automatic functions, including sleep. We usually don't sleep enough. Besides unstable mood responses, lack of sleep impacts the whole system. Among many biological responses, skin ages quicker (less restoring collagen produced at night), memory is lost (not processed well in hippocampus during deep sleep), and weight is gained (elevation of peptide ghrelin which stimulates hunger).

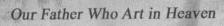

Brainstem
Midbrain
Pons
Medulla
Basilar artery
Vertebral arteries

Our Father Who Art in Heaven

I honor You for deciding one third
of my day should be spent at rest, asleep.

When I don't sleep, so many of the
systems You have designed to work
while I rest, do not interact as well.
Even knowing how to see Your will on
this earth becomes clouded,
as earthly issues are all I can see.

Forgive me for keeping my life at such
a pace of busy, that my sleep suffers.
And then anxiety is my sleep partner, instead
of Your perfect peace that surpasses all under-
standing. Thank You for helping me come to
acceptance for Your work in my life, so I can
see a picture of me at peace, as I prepare to sleep.

For Thine is the kingdom, and the power,
and the glory forever and ever. Amen!

ZZZ Sleep ZZZ

We spend about one third of our lives asleep. And now we spend hours a day staring at screens of light. This can confuse the circadian rhythms, which are triggered by light. Can't sleep? Turn off that screen!

"In peace I will both lie down and sleep, for You alone, O Lord, make me to dwell in safety."
Psalm 4:8 NASB

A Prayer for Another
To the Maker of the Brain Stem, The Counselor*

As I learn the parts of the brain stem with names like the pons medulla oblongata, created for the automatic functions related to breathing, heart rate and blood pressure, Lord I think of _____.
[name of family member, friend, co-worker]
I can see the constant stress impacting these automatic systems, and there is trouble in their body because of it.

In Your name as their Mighty Counselor, I pray for _____'s brain stem: for a regulation in sleeping to allow healing. May they feel Your perfect peace thinking about sleeping, falling asleep, during sleep, and waking up! Amen!

*Isaiah 9:6

brain stem ~ b

asleep!

medulla
oblongata

brain stem

instinctively

brain stem

It houses a part of the Automatic Nervous System in the medulla oblongata. This system is divided into the parasympathetic (dampening) and sympathetic (quick) response systems, often working independently. And sometimes working in tandem, such as automatically keeping the heart beating.

Our Father Who Art in Heaven

It is amazing to think how You created this heart
of mine to beat so many times in a minute,
providing such vital things for my brain.
Thank You for my medulla oblongata,
even if just because it is fun to say.

Yet, I let my stress and my perceptions
keep my heart in such a state of alert,
forcing it to work so much harder.

Forgive me for not caring about my heart enough,
for not noticing the tension messages
in my sympathetic nervous system.
Create in me a clean heart, Oh Lord, and
heal my heart from damage caused already.

**For Thine is the kingdom, and the power,
and the glory forever and ever. Amen!**

heart
breathing
pain
awake
touch
consciousness

brain stem

"Create in me a clean heart, O God,
and renew a steadfast spirit within me...."
Psalm 51:10 NASB

a beating machine

The average human heart, beating at 72 beats per minute, will beat approximately 2.5 billion times during an average 66-year life span. It weighs approximately 9 to 11 ounces in females and 11 to 12 ounces in males.

involuntary

A Prayer for Another
Maker of the Brain Stem, My Strength and Song*

I can feel my heart beat increase when I go from
a state of rest to a state of alarm. I think today of
_____
[name of family member, friend, co-worker]
that I know lives in such states of alarm all of the time.

In Your name as their strength and song,
I pray for _____'s medulla oblongata and
the parasympathetic system You designed
to counteract the stress responses.
May You be their strength in life situations that
they are trying to handle by themselves.

Bring a song to their mind today, a song of peace, so
that _____'s joy may be in You,
even in the hardest of times. Amen!
* Isaiah 12:2

brain stem

brain stem – c

panic &

breathing

Your marvelous brain and body have two nervous systems at work all the time. One is made to get excited (sympathetic), and one is to relax you (parasympathetic). If the excite is overworked, the limbic system trains your brain to panic: fright, flight time. Learning to breathe well retrains it!

Our Father Who Art in Heaven

Lord, I believe that having two part nervous system response is part of Your doing Your will on this earth through me.

Forgive me for often being in the frame of mind of anxiety and excitement. I have worn out the gift of my alert response system, and so I panic, or I avoid topics completely.

Help me to notice more quickly when my body is clearly showing me that my feeling and thinking are not in perfect order as designed. Help me to use the balance of my nervous systems, and my best breathing to feel less of me and more of You. Help me rest in You.

For Thine is the kingdom, and the power, and the glory forever and ever. Amen!

trigger
oxygen
carbon
dioxide
heart
rate
anxiety
peace

Nervous System

Brain
Cerebellum
Spinal cord
Brachial plexus
Intercostal nerves
Musculocutaneous nerve
Radial nerve
Subcostal nerve
Lumbar plexus
Median nerve
Iliohypogastric nerve
Sacral plexus
Genitofemoral nerve
Obturator nerve
Femoral nerve
Pudendal nerve
Sciatic nerve
Ulnar nerve
Muscular branches of femoral nerve
Saphenous nerve
Tibial nerve
Common peroneal nerve
Deep peroneal nerve
Superficial peroneal nerve

"Be anxious for nothing, but in everything by prayer and supplication with thanksgiving let your request be made known to God. And the peace of God, which surpassess all comprehension, shall guard your hearts and YOUR MINDS in Christ Jesus."
Philippians 4:6-7 NASB

patrol car = panic

"After my teenage son's unexpected arrest, when a sheriff car would pass me, I learned what panic attacks were. I began to fear sheriff cars, even when there was none in sight. In learning about breathing, and giving my brain it's best oxygen to examine what was really wrong (fear of probation or court), I retrained my brain ...breathe well... and make a picture of what I would look in acceptance of what had happened. And after much practice, even began to bless the officer in that car as it passed." - Karen D. Wood

patrol cars

A Prayer for Another
To the Maker of the My Nervous Systems, My Refiner*

Thank you Lord for the connections between brain and body to excite and calm down. But Lord, I know _____ [name of family member, friend, co-worker] is controlled by fear and terrible reactions of panic. So, they react impulsively to protect themselves, or they just shut down and withdraw. Panic is their constant companion, with breathing out of control.

Be with _____, and their breathing even today Lord. Cause them to first think of You, and to notice their breathing. Instead of overwhelming thoughts of panic and fear, help them to combine thoughts of You with strong breathing,

As their Refiner, please fine tune the connections between their panic and You! Amen!   *Malachi 8:8

lungs + diaphragm
breathing

delightful

breathing

9-16
breaths per minute at rest
?-27
breaths per minute in a panic attack:
light headedness, numbness,
sense of need for flight or frantic

Our Father Who Art in Heaven

*The systems that work inside of me
automatically are truly miraculous, and
I praise Your name as the originator of them!*

*The intake of oxygen and the exhale of
waste products from my system is a process
I have rewired in my response to situations
and stress. Forgive me for not using a vital tool
that was a gift from You: the ability
to communicate with the automatic system.*

*Help me be aware of when my breathing is
not at a healthy rate for my organs and my brain.
Allow me to see the picture of what I would
look like if I was breathing well.*
**For Thine is the kingdom, and the power,
and the glory forever and ever. Amen!**

trigger
oxygen
carbon
dioxide
heart
rate

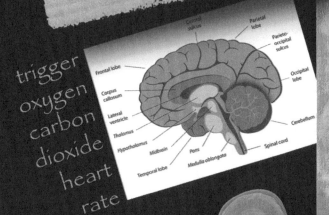

paradox of physiology

*"When you hyperventilate,
you inhale too much oxygen, which
decreased carbon dioxide in your blood
stream. Oxygen binds tightly to hemo-
globin, which results in less oxyen being
released in the tissues and the extremities.
The paradox is that even though you
inhaled too much oxygen, less is available
to your tissues."*

- John B. Arden, *Rewire Your Brain*, page 38.

breathing
*"Let everything that has breath
praise the Lord." Psalm 150:6 NASB*

diaphragm!

Wait - where is the prayer? In my therapy practice, I am spending more time now teaching best breathing, for more oxygen to those brain parts you have been praying for. So, here are a few tips to retrain your brain to breathe!

2. EXHALE for 4-10 seconds through a small hole in your mouth. Imagine the diaphragm as an air bag deflating, pushing up your lungs. You should feel your ribs go down. It may feel very strange at first; try laying on the floor, as it is easier to watch your ribs as the diaphragm fills and deflates underneath.

Take a few regular breaths, and try again!

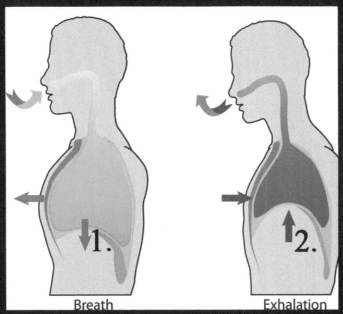

Breath   Exhalation

1. INHALE through your nose. To breathe correctly, it has nothing to do with shoulder action (which is how we breathe in panic), but the diaphragm filling like a bag downward, pulling your lungs down, and filling it like a balloon. Touch your lower ribs while you breathe, as they'll expand if you are filling that diaphragm! Try inhaling 4-10 seconds.

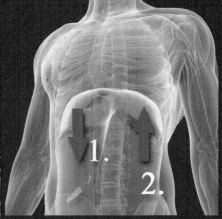

breathing
lungs + diaphragm

breathing & meditation

Mindfulness meditation is one of the recent new terms for everything from yoga, to spiritual focus in meditation. The practice of quieting the mind to focus on Our Creator is not a new concept, has immense health benefits, and the brain function involved is understood more in the last decade.

Our Father Who Art in Heaven

To call upon Your name while I quiet my racing mind, is the most powerful way to become internally and externally at rest, to hear from You.

The design of all of my brain being impacted by meditation - focused attention - is to put on You and Your will on this earth far above all of the worries and fears that fill my mind.

Forgive me for the every day things in life that fill my schedule, so that my anterior cingulate, prefontal lobes, thalamus, amygdala, hippocampus, temporal and occipital lobes, breathing systems, sleep centers.... all don't get the chemical reactions and best state of mind thinking while I seek Your face.
For Thine is the kingdom, and the power, and the glory forever and ever. Amen!

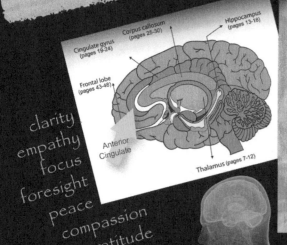

Cingulate gyrus (pages 19-24)
Corpus callosum (pages 25-30)
Hippocampus (pages 13-18)
Frontal lobe (pages 43-48)
Anterior Cingulate
Thalamus (pages 7-12)

clarity
empathy
focus
foresight
peace
compassion
gratitude
humility
acceptance
the mind of Christ

"Let the words of my mouth, and the meditation of my heart be acceptable in Thy sight, O Lord, my rock and my redeemer." Psalm 19:14 NASB

Internal & Eternal Attunement

"There are particular brain regions that are emphasized by practicing mindful meditation. The middle of the prefrontal cortex is involved in self-observation ... A state of positive attention made possible by the left frontal lobe combines with tactile sensations...decisions, empathy, and emotion (the front of the cingulate cortex). - J, Arden, *Rewire Your Brain*, page 202.

meditation

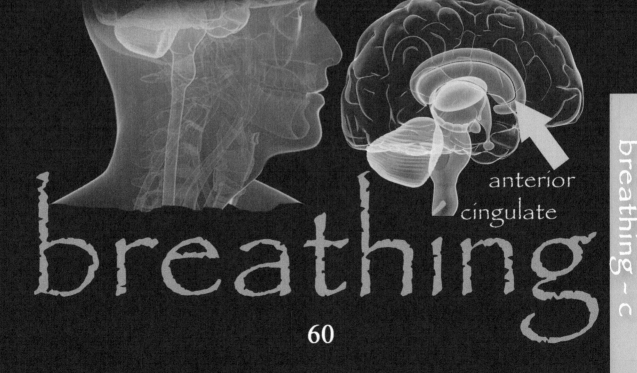

A Prayer for Another
To the Maker of the My Nervous Systems, My Redeemer*

As I quiet myself and allow my anterior cingulate to receive more oxygen and balance my thinking, I know _____ [name of family member, friend, co-worker] is feeling frantically out of control. If they let themselves slow down at all, their thoughts race and emotions escalate.

Today I intercede for their whole limbic system of emotional reaction to be balanced with their frontal cortex systems, so they can find balance in You as their Redeemer. Let them even feel the difference in their blinking (less eye tension) and how they breathe. Amen!   *Isaiah 59:20

frontal cortex

anterior cingulate

breathing

60

breathing ~ c

About the

"Karen is an energetic individual with an instantly practical ability to see an overview of the situation before her and the obvious next steps to take toward freeing progress.

"She is engaged, personal, thought provoking, compassionate, understanding, encouraging, and unafraid to challenge her clients to new frontiers of great effectiveness in life and relationships.

"She is fabulous with teaching clients about their brain processing, helping them to think about their thinking and apply new skills in difficult situations.

"There is instinctively that knowledge upon meeting with Karen that she helps me past places I have not known how to move though until now."

~ Lois Griffith, LMFT, Clear Thinking Counseling Alliance

"Over the past few years, Karen Wood has been invaluable to the P.A.I.N. organization from both a professional and personal standpoint. Her commitment to helping others in need is beyond anything I've seen. Not only do I consider her a trusted colleague, I am proud to call her my friend."

- Flindt Andersen. Founder & Executive Director
P.A.I.N., Prescription Abusers In Need, gotPAINusa.com

"The path of the righteous is like the dawn that shines brighter and brighter until the full day." Proverbs 4:18 NASB

Author

Karen Dawn Wood is a Licensed Clinical Social Worker
in private practice as a Brain Trainer and Behavioral Counselor.

Backgound:
- B.A. in Fine Arts, California State University Hayward
- Masters in Social Work, California State University Fresno
- Licensed Clinical Social Worker, State of California
- Worked as a social worker in foster care and a group home, where the clarity came
  that teaching brain and behavior allowed kids/parents to achieve more success.
- Became certified in Outcome Based Thinking, and continued exploration of
  incorporating brain functioning in counseling.

Current Work:
- Founder of the Clear Thinking Counseling Alliance (CTCA), a group of
  therapists and counselors committed to training together to help clients
  discover how to access their best states of mind.
- Developing concept of "art thinking," using drawing to explore reactions,
  brain processing and viewing of self in the future.
- Co-facilitator for four years of a weekly support group for parents with
  addicted children/adults, through Prescription Abusers in Need **(gotPAINUSA.com)**.
- Writing more books on *Brain Prayers* (for specific topics, i.e., brain on drugs, PTSD).
- Speaking on brain, breathing & behavior.

Personal:
- Married to Russell for thirty years, with two adult sons, Drew and Parker.
- On national Board of Directors for Assemblies of God Marriage Encounter
  (you deserve a weekend! **agme.org**).
- Voracious appetite for dark chocolate, reading anything about the brain, and
  biographies of the journeys of people doing faith, trauma and joy.

brainprayers.com

62

Q: what do I read next?

PRAYER

BIBLE

BEHAVIOR

NEUROLOGY

Brain Prayers contains all four topics, with the prayers, the Bible verses, impact on behavior, and introductory neurology.

Amen, Daniel G. ***Change Your Brain, Change Your Life, The Breakthrough Program for Conquering Anxiety, Depression, Obsessiveness, Anger, and Impulsiveness.*** Three Rivers Press (Random House), 1998. Anything from this pioneering neuropsychiatrist in brain scanning is loaded with practical ways to change the brain and behavior.

Amen, Daniel G. ***Healing the Hardware of the Soul, Enhance Your Brain to Improve Your Work, Love, and Spiritual Life.*** *Atria Books, 2008.* A program allowing transformation of the mind - the seat of the soul - for greater self-understanding.

Amthor, Frank. ***Neuroscience for Dummies***. John Wiley & Sons, Canada, 2010. This is authored by a professor of psychology, who holds appointments in departments of neurobiology, optometry and biomedical engineering, and explains brain structure and function in smaller topics with graphics.

Arden, John B. and Linford, Lloyd. ***Brain-Based Therapy for Adults; Evidence-Based Treatment for Everyday Practice.*** John Wiley & Sons, 2009. Brain based therapeutic strategy book, which is a great partner with client reading Arden's Rewire Your Brain referenced below.

Arden, John. ***Rewire Your Brain: Think Your Way to a Better Life.*** John Wiley & Sons, 2010. A great-place-to-start book in understanding more about brain function and practical insights on behavior: cells that fire together, wire together? Extensive resource list by chapter topic.

A: resource ideas & bibliography

Beuregard, Mario and O'Leary, Denyse. *The Spiritual Brain: A Neuroscientist's Case for the Existence of the Soul.* Harper One, 2008. Studying and scanning nuns, this neuroscientist and journalist explore the brain and what happens exploring beyond self.

Brizendine, Louann. *The Female Brain.* Harmony, 2007. The result of this neuropsychiatrist's research on the development of females in all phases of life, creating "lean, mean, communicating machines." Easy to read.

Brizendine, Louann. *The Male Brain: A Breakthrough Understanding of How Men and Boys Think.* Harmony, 2011. A follow up to The Female Brain, walking through every phase of life of the "lean, mean, problem solving machine" brain. The beginning to end review was very helpful for this female!

Carter, Rita. *The Human Brain Book: an Illustrated Guide to its Structure, Function, and Disorders.* DK, 2009. A graphic feast of 250 large pages of brain information in bite-sized pieces, with a DVD. Very reasonably priced for a large treasure.

Doidge, Norman. *The Brain that Changes Itself: Stories of Personal Triumph from the Frontiers of Brain Science.* Viking, 2007. Case studies of hopeful protraits of the changing brain by this psychiatrist and researcher.

Hass-Coehn, Noah and Carr, Richard. *Art Therapy and Clinical Neuroscience.* Jessica Kingsley Publishers, London, 2008. A series of articles exploring relationships between art, creativity, and interpersonal neurobiology.

Holley, Mary F. *Crystal Meth: They Call It Ice.* Tate Publishing, 2005. This physician lost a younger brother to this drug, and wrote this complete and complex book, including the impact of drugs in the brain. She boldly speaks of God's love and the power of prayer, knowing that only the Holy Spirit can speak to the mind of an addict. She even has "Nerd Boxes" for us geeky, brain curious people. Excellent resource lists.

Horstman, Judith. *The Scientific American Day in the Life of Your Brain, A 24 Hour Journal of What's Happening in Your Brain as You Sleep, Dream, Wake Up, Eat, Work, Play, Fight, Love, Worry, Compete, Hope, Make Important Decisions, Age, and Change.* Jossey-Bass, A Wiley Imprint, 2009. My fascination with brain and behavior started with a Scientific American article on ADHD in 1997. They always do a great job with books on the brain. This book's title says it all in a little more description than titles usually get!

"Instruct the wise and they will be wiser still;
teach the righteous and they will add to their learning." NLT Proverbs 9:9

resource ideas & bibliography

PRAYER   BIBLE

BEHAVIOR   NEUROLOGY

Henslin, Earl. ***This is Your Brain on Joy, A Revolutionary Program for Balancing Mood, Restoring Brain Health, and Nurturing Spiritual Growth.*** Thomas Nelson, 2008. When my computer was stolen the week the first draft of the book you hold was to be submitted to the publisher, Dr. Henslin's book was one of the treasures also stolen in the computer bag. My much highlighted copy was like a friend lost. It is a look into five mood centers of the brain, and how to find more balance and joy. Even in retyping this book!

Howard, Pierce J. ***The Owner's Manual for The Brain: Everyday Applications from Mind-Brain Research.*** A Bard Press Book, Third Edition, 2009. Several inches thick, full of topics and applications. Not a graphic presentation, but loaded with practical information.

Hurlburt, Charles E. and Horton, T.C. ***Wonderful Names of Our Wonderful Lord: Names and Titles of the Lord Jesus Christ as Found in the Old and New Testament.*** Abridged Edition. Barbour Publishing, Ohio, 2002. A little book filled with many names and descriptions.

LeDoux, Joseph. ***The Emotional Brain: The Mysterious Underpinnings of Emotional Life.*** Simon & Schuster Paperbacks, 1996. This leading researcher in neuroscience explores brain mechanisms underlying emotion, designed to be read by the lay person. He also has a band called The Amygdaloids...cracks me up.

LeDoux, Joseph. ***Synaptic Self: How Our Brains Become Who We Are.*** Penguin Books, 2002. A closer look at synapses, the spaces between the neurons, how that makes our personality, and who we are as humans.

"The proverbs of Solomon son of David, king of Israel:
for gaining wisdom and instruction; for understanding words of insight;
for receiving instruction in prudent behavior, doing what is right and just and fair;
for giving prudence to those who are simple, knowledge and discretion to the young—
let the wise listen and add to their learning, and let the discerning get guidance
... for understanding proverbs and parables, the sayings and riddles of the wise....

resource ideas & bibliography

MacBeth, Sybil. *Praying In Color: Drawing a New Path to God (active prayer series).* Paraclete Press,2007. An exploration into drawing prayers with colored markers in hand. Doodling meets the Maker of all creativity to keep the mind focused. Written by a mathematician, dancer, and pastor's wife (I just love that combination!). Also has a version for kids, and black and white version for men.

Medina, John. *Brain Rules: 12 Principles for Surviving and Thriving at Work, Home, and School.* Pear Press, 2008. A developmental molecular biologist writes each chapter about a brain rule, and a reminder from his two-year old about the marvel of curiosity.

Newberg, Andrew and Waldman, Mark. *How God Changes Your Brain: Breakthrough Findings from A Leading Neurologist.* Ballantine, 2010. A neuroscientist and therapist exploring multiple faiths and brain scans, discovering much about the impact of meditation and prayer on the brain.

Omartian, Stormie. *The Power of Prayer to Change Your Marriage.* Harvest House Publishers, 2009. This is one in a series of books of prayers that have been read by millions.

Pinel, John P.J. with Edwards, Maggie. *Anatomy of the Human Brain, Second Edition. A Brain and Psychology Coloring Book.* Pearson Education, 2008. A step up in the technical understanding of brain function, in coloring page format.

Ramachandran, V.S, qne Blakeslee, Sandra. *Phantoms in the Brain: Probing the Mysteries of the Human Mind.* Harper, 1998. This professor was named by Newsweek as one of the hundred most important people to watch in the next century, writing with a science writer on his own experiences with neurological patients.

Siegel, Daniel. *The Developing Mind: How Relationships and the Brain Interact to Shape Who We Are.* Guilford Press, 2001, 2012. The term "interpersonal neurobiology" was put on the map by this child psychiatrist, on how our interaction with children shapes their brains and minds.

Yerkovich, Milan and Kay. *How We Love: Discover Your Love Style, Enhance Your Marriage.* Waterbrook Press, 2008. They draw on the powerful tool of attachment theory to show how your early life experiences created an "intimacy imprint"– an underlying blueprint that shapes your behavior, beliefs, and expectations of all relationships, especially your marriage. An excellent read for putting the "fun" back in dysfunction to rewire the brain.

The fear of the Lord is the beginning of knowledge, but fools despise wisdom and instruction."
Proverbs 1:1-7   NASB

author & subject

index

The Author acknowledges the following for the images used in this book.

Key: a=above, b=below/bottom, c=center, f=full, l=left, r=right

Cover - a: ©istock.com file 10713237, modified. b: ©istock.com, file 303161, modified.
Intro i (r) contents - f: neuron color ©istock.com file 2789321, modified.
Intro ii (l) brain map - f: neuron b&w ©istock.com file 14137482 modified, c: ©istock.com file 5664112, modified. b: ©istock.com file 5809739, modified. r: ©istock.com file 5383354, modified.
Intro iii (r) brain map - f: see intro ii. c: dreamstock.com file 11898161, Sebastian Kaulitzki.
          b: ©istock.com file 11224556, modified.
Intro iv (l), v (r) this book - f: same as intro I. cardboard ©istock.com file 5306609.
Intro vi (l), vii (r) each page - see pages 1 and 2.

Images on each prayer page - a: cardboard ©istock.com file 5306609. c: Adobe Photoshop background image "blue wash," modified. c: neuron color ©istock.com file 2789321, modified.
          a: cardboard: ©istock.com file 5306609.
Page 1 (l) amygdala a - l: Wikimedia Commons, file amygdala.png from Anatomography, website maintained by Life Science Databases (LSDB), modified.
          b: ©istock.com file 26276259, modified.
Page 2 (r) amygdala a - f: ©Science Source Image Number: SN0002, Roger Harris.
Page 3 (l) amygdala b - l: Wikimedia Commons file amygdala.png from Anatomography, website maintained by Life Science Databases (LSDB), modified.
          b: ©istock.com file 11224556, modified.
Page 4 (r) amygdala b - f: ©istock.com file 24009093, modified.
Page 5 (l) amygdala c - l: ©dreamstock.com ID 12972630 Gnanavel Subramani, modified.
          b: ©istock.com file 11224556, modified.
Page 6 (r) amygdala c - c: Wikimedia Commons file amygdala.png from Anatomography, website maintained byLife Science Databases (LSDB), modified.
          b: ©istock.com file 11224556, modified.
Page 7 (l) thalamus a - l: ©dreamstock.com ID 21770731, modified.
          b: ©istock.com file 11224556, modified.
Page 8 (r) thalamus a - f: ©dreamstock.com ID Sebastian Kaulitzki, modified.
Page 9 (l) thalamus b - l: Wikimedia Commons file hippolobes.gif National Institute of Health.

"I thank my God every time I remember you. In all my prayers for all of you, I always pray with joy because of your partnership in the gospel from the first day until now, being confident of this, that He who began a good work in you will carry it on to completion until the day of Christ Jesus."
Philippians 1:3 NASB

May these pages expand your prayers as you explore your brain, and explode how you see God at work on this earth, richly blessing your life!

CPSIA information can be obtained at www.ICGtesting.com
Printed in the USA
BVOW10s0328280714

360556BV00002B/2/P